BAYONET-FENCING

AND

SWORD-PRACTICE.

BY

ALFRED HUTTON,

LATE CAPTAIN KING'S DRAGOON GUARDS.

1882.

(*All rights reserved.*)

The Naval & Military Press Ltd

Published by the
The Naval & Military Press
in association with the Royal Armouries

Unit 10 Ridgewood Industrial Park,
Uckfield, East Sussex, TN22 5QE
Tel: +44 (0) 1825 749494
Fax: +44 (0) 1825 765701

MILITARY HISTORY AT YOUR FINGERTIPS
www.naval-military-press.com

ONLINE GENEALOGY RESEARCH
www.military-genealogy.com

ONLINE MILITARY CARTOGRAPHY
www.militarymaproom.com

ROYAL ARMOURIES

The Library & Archives Department at the Royal Armouries Museum, Leeds, specialises in the history and development of armour and weapons from earliest times to the present day. Material relating to the development of artillery and modern fortifications is held at the Royal Armouries Museum, Fort Nelson.

For further information contact:
Royal Armouries Museum, Library, Armouries Drive,
Leeds, West Yorkshire LS10 1LT
Royal Armouries, Library, Fort Nelson, Down End Road, Fareham PO17 6AN

Or visit the Museum's website at
www.armouries.org.uk

In reprinting in facsimile from the original, any imperfections are inevitably reproduced and the quality may fall short of modern type and cartographic standards.

PREFACE.

As there appears to be a desire for a re-issue of my system of Bayonet-fencing, I have thought it expedient to combine the matter contained in my two former treatises, 'Swordsmanship and Bayonet-fencing,' and 'The Cavalry Swordsman,' from which, after careful revision, I have eliminated certain matter not required for fencing-room work, and have added one or two exercises which seem to me to be of importance.

It must be clearly understood that this system pertains distinctly to the fencing-room, and is not in any way applicable to the parade-ground.

ALFRED HUTTON.

ARMY AND NAVY CLUB,
April, 1882.

BAYONET-FENCING AND SWORD-PRACTICE.

SMALL-SWORD fencing is undoubtedly the basis of all exercise for hand-to-hand weapons; since, however, the Army already possesses a work on the subject, I shall not discuss that branch of the swordsman's art further than to call my readers' attention to the guards therein used, to which I shall have to make allusion in the following pages.

The guards in fencing are seven in number, as follows:—

1. *Quarte* . . { Turn the nails of the right hand upwards, carrying the hand very slightly to the left. This guards a high thrust inside the blade,

2. *Tierce* . . { Turn the back of the hand upwards and guard to the right. This guards a high thrust outside.

3. *Half-circle* { Turn the nails up, raise the hand a little, drop the point about as low as the opponent's groin, and guard to the left. This guards a low thrust inside.

4. *Seconde* . { Turn the back of the hand up, drop the point as in 3, and guard to the right. This guards a low thrust outside.

5. *Prime* . . { Turn the back of the hand up, carry the hand to the left about as high as the shoulder, the point as in 3 and 4. This guards an inside thrust.

In *High Prime* the hand is raised as high as the forehead.

6. *Quinte* . . { Is formed in the same manner as 3, guarding to the right. This has the same effect as 4.

7. *Quarte outside.* { Formed like quarte, but guarding to the right. This has the same effect as 2. It is a most useful guard.

BAYONET-FENCING.

In forming a plan of attack and defence for a military weapon such as this, it must be borne in mind to what class of persons the exercise is to be adapted. It is not intended for the amusement of the select few who frequent our London fencing-rooms, but for the general use of the infantry soldier, and must therefore be, as far as possible, devoid of technical terms; its cuts, guards, and points must be as few as possible, and it must be rendered so simple in its details as to be within the comprehension of the dullest recruit.

Towards attaining to proficiency in the use of any hand-to-hand weapon, it is most essential that the

(7)

learner should be taught to assume a firm and easy position; one which will allow the action of all his limbs to be perfectly free from restraint, and his weapon (which is, *in this case*, a heavy one) to be as much as possible under his command.

In assuming the position of "*Guard*," the feet should be kept well apart, the space between them being regulated by the height of the man, the knees well bent, so as to be ready for motion in any direction, the body upright, but not stiff, and its weight equally distributed between the legs, so that there should be no more strain upon one than upon the other.

In order to give the soldier the most complete command of his bayonet, he should be taught to hold the weapon in such a manner that the centre of gravity or balance should be in the left hand, the right hand of course grasping the small of the butt.

Lesson 1.

Charge Bayonets.

Guard . . . Fall back to the second position as above described, the left hand grasping the musket where it balances, the right hand grasping the small, with the wrist lightly touching the hip. The point of the bayonet should be opposite the right breast of the opponent.

Prove distance Extend the arms and body until the point touches the opponent's right breast, at the same time bracing the right knee.

Guard . . . As before.

Points.

1st Point . . { Advance the musket smartly towards the part aimed at, as far as the arms and extension of the right leg can reach.

Point in Tierce { Turn the musket-sling uppermost, raise the butt and hand as high as the ear, the back of the hand being towards the ear, and advance the point as far as the arms and extension can reach.

The Throw { In making this point the grip of the left hand is slackened, so as to allow the musket to glide through it. It should not be used as a rule, but only exceptionally, as occasion requires. I do not approve of quitting the grip with the left hand entirely, as it renders the bayoneteer liable to be disarmed.

Guards.

The guards are four in number.

1st . . . . . { Keep the point high, and pass the musket slightly to the right. This guards a high point made inside the musket.

2nd . . . . { Keep the point high, and pass the musket slightly to the left. This guards a high point outside.

(9)

3rd . . . . { Drop the point, and pass the musket slightly to the right. This guards a low point inside.

4th. . . . . { Drop the point, turning the sling uppermost, and pass the musket slightly to the left. This guards a low point outside.

All guards should be made with that part of the musket which is immediately above the left hand, and which corresponds to the forte of a sword.

Lesson 2.

BEATS.

The beats are intended to force an opening previously to making a point; they are formed from, and numbered according to the four guards, by lightly striking the adversary's blade, forcing the musket down it.

FEINTS.

The best feints are the following:—

Disengage . . { Pass the point of the bayonet round, underneath and close to the musket of the opponent, and point. This is done to take advantage of some opening left by the opponent.

One, two . .	Pass the bayonet under and close to the musket of the opponent, as in "Disengage," then bring the bayonet back again to its original position, and point.
Cut over . .	Pass the point over that of the opponent, and point.

Cut over and disengage.
Beat and disengage.
Beat and one, two.
Disengage, beat, and disengage.

Care should be taken that the hand should be gradually advanced all the time that the feint is being executed, so that feint and point should be one continued movement.

Lesson 3.

THE RETURN.

The most effective blow that can be given is a *return hit*, delivered immediately after the opponent's attack is parried and before he has had time to recover to his guard. With a view to enabling the beginner to "return" with precision, the following lesson will be found effective.

1. (A) Front rank—Point.
    Rear rank—Guard 1, point.
   (B) Front rank—Point.
    Rear rank—Guard 1, disengage, and point.

2. (A) Front rank—Disengage and point.
   Rear rank—Guard 2, point.
   (B) Front rank—Disengage and point.
   Rear rank—Guard 2, disengage, and point.
3. Front rank—Point low (inside).
   Rear rank—Guard 3, return high.
4. (A) Front rank—Point low (outside).
   Rear rank—Guard 4, return low, sling uppermost.
   (B) Front rank—Point low (outside).
   Rear rank—Guard 4, return high, sling down.

PRACTICES.

The practices are a combination of various points and guards, intended to give the pupil a good method of attack, defence, and return, and so to prepare him for loose play.

They will be performed at first by word of command, and, when the men thoroughly understand them, judging their own time, the points and guards must be executed as rapidly as possible.

1st Practice.

Front Rank.	*Rear Rank.*
Point (inside high).	Guard 1, point (inside high).
Guard 1, point (inside low).	Guard 3, point (inside high).
Guard 1.	

2ND PRACTICE.

Front Rank.	*Rear Rank.*
Disengage and point (outside).	Guard 2, point (high outside).
Guard 2, point (outside low).	Guard 4, point tierce (high).
Guard 2.	

3RD PRACTICE.

Rear rank engages with his point horizontal or low.

Beat 3, point (inside high).	Guard 1, point (inside low).
Guard 3, point (inside high).	Guard 1, point in tierce (high inside).
Guard 1.	

4TH PRACTICE.

Disengage and point.	Guard 2, point.
Guard 3 (raising right hand a little), retire at same moment, and return with the throw.	

THE BUTT.

Our soldiers have never yet been taught any method of using the *butt* to advantage; still under certain circumstances it is the only effectual attack that can be made. It is useful when the combatants are so

(13)

close to one another that it is impossible for either to disentangle his point, which must often occur in a *mêlée*, and does so sometimes even in fencing-room practice.

There are four strokes with the butt, two in front and two behind.

1. Raise the muzzle, and force the toe of the butt smartly into the pit of the opponent's stomach.
2. Throw back the muzzle, and thrust the heel-plate full into the opponent's face. This will be found an effective *finish* after inflicting No. 1.
3. Bring the right foot forward, and at the same moment deliver the toe of the butt sharply behind the left ear.
4. In case of the opponent's arm being raised so as to make it difficult to reach his head, bring the right foot forward, and deliver the toe of the butt sharply below the ribs and a little to the opponent's rear. This will have the same practical effect as No. 1.

STOPS.

To prevent confusion between these defences and the guards against point, I have named them as above.

1. Hold the musket nearly horizontal, lower it, and stop No. 1 with the stock between the hands.

(14)

2. Hold the musket nearly horizontal, raise it, and force up the opponent's butt with the stock between the hands.

3. Lower the butt with the musket nearly perpendicular, and stop 3 with the stock above the left hand.

4. Lower the butt, and stop 4 with the stock between the hands.

RETURNS.

1. Stop 1, return 3 at face, over the musket, without stepping forward.

2. Stop 2, and return 3 at face, or 1 at ribs.

3. Stop 3 and return 1.

4. Stop 4 and return 3 at face, over the musket.

Different returns may of course be made according to the position of the opponent.

LOOSE PLAY.

In loose play the right hand should always be free of the side.

When a hit is received the party receiving it should acknowledge by dropping the point of his bayonet to the ground; the party giving the hit to come to the engaging guard.

In engaging with an opponent with whose style you are unacquainted, allow him to attack first; you will by that means learn the faults of his play, and make sure of your own hit by a smart " return," after guarding his attack.

It should be carefully impressed upon the soldier that when engaging with a man armed with a bayonet, he must never press or bear heavily on the weapon of his antagonist; for were such to be the case, the opponent would disengage, and thereby take away the support from his bayonet, when his point would fall to one side and he would be completely open to his antagonist's attack.

All hits from the knee upwards are to be counted.

THE SWORD-BAYONET.

The sword-bayonet is undoubtedly superior to the ordinary triangular-bladed weapon, for the reason that its cutting-edges offer increased variety and facility in the return, but in fencing with it the soldier must be thoroughly impressed with the fact that his attack must always be commenced with the point, for should he attempt to lead off with a cut, the act of slightly raising his weapon to effect it would lay him open to the thrust of his opponent.

The points, guards against point, and strokes with the butt, are precisely the same as those laid down for the ordinary bayonet.

(16)

I have named the cuts and their corresponding guards by letters of the alphabet in order to distinguish them from the guards against point.

Cuts.

There are five cuts admissible in the use of the sword-bayonet.

Cut A. . . . { At the left side of the head, is made by advancing the blade smartly, and striking with the back edge, downward in a diagonal direction, and at the same time drawing the weapon back, so as to give free play to the edge.

Cut B. . . . { At the right side of the head, striking diagonally downward, with the real edge; and making the drawing cut as above.

Cut C. . . . { At the outside of the left knee; the stroke being effected diagonally upwards from right to left—striking with the back.

Cut D. . . . { At the inside of the knee, with the true edge diagonally upwards from left to right.

Cut E. . . . { Perpendicularly at the head, the cut to be made with the true edge.

(17)

GUARDS.

Guard A .. { Slightly raise the point and receive cut A on the back edge, as near the cross-guard as possible.

Guard B .. { Raise the point and receive cut B on the true edge, near the cross-guard.

Guard C .. { Raise the point and drop the *butt* to the left front, receiving cut C on the butt below the right hand.

Guard D .. { Raise the point and drop the butt to the right front, turning the lock-plate to the rear in so doing, and receive cut D on the butt, below the right hand.

Guard E .. { Raise the musket above the head, sling upwards, the muzzle to the left, and receive cut E on the stock, between the hands.

Should the low cut C or D be made as a direct attack, it may be guarded with 3 or 4; but if made as a return the guard with the butt will be found indispensable.

The low guards C and D have been objected to on account of the danger of receiving a blow on the right hand, but the persons who objected to them were unable to suggest any improvement, and I myself after careful investigation have found it impossible to formulate any more effective guard.

It must be carefully impressed on the soldier that a cut with the sword-bayonet is only admissible as a return; and then not as a rule, but merely to be used as occasion may require. The point is to be preferred as being more effective and, in most instances, quicker.

SWORD-PRACTICE.

In teaching the young soldier to become thoroughly proficient in the use of his weapon, two main points ought to be considered. First, the best means of affording him sufficient suppleness of wrist and quickness of eye to enable him to play his sword to advantage; and secondly—a point which is of equal importance—how to give him the necessary strength of arm for sustaining the weight of it with as little fatigue as possible during a heavy day's work.

The sabre ought, during the hours of practice—of independent practice I mean—to be represented by a weapon in weight, length, and shape, as nearly similar to the real one as possible. The weapon I allude to is the steel practice-sword (those made by Wilkinson are the best and most durable).

It may be objected that the practice-sword is a dangerous weapon to place in a soldier's hand; be it remembered then, that when men use it they are always encased in padded defensive armour, so that there is hardly as much real risk in the practice-sword as there is in the singlestick; I have used the former regularly for some time as matter of preference, and I have never yet seen a serious accident happen with it.

The exercise of *fencing* with the foil, the representative of the rapier, has been recommended for the soldier as being *the basis of all good swordsmanship*. This is true, but it is only the basis of his work; he really has to learn the efficient use of a heavy sabre, so let us glance at the nature of small-sword fencing, and consider what relation it bears to the actual practical work which he has to master. Fencing is a most difficult and delicate exercise, and one which takes a lifetime to learn thoroughly; it requires a keen eye, a firm, yet supple wrist, and a touch almost as light as that of an artist's brush. These attributes may be acquired, and often are, under the tuition of a first-rate master, but, unfortunately, the army cannot command the services of an Angelo in its regimental schools, so we must take fencing as it is at present taught in the army, and according to that standard rate its value to the soldier.

The main effect of fencing is to gymnasticise the pupil into the best position of body and limbs for commanding his sword; to impart to him a knowledge and appreciation of the point, the most deadly attack of the sword; and also to give him, after much practice, quickness of eye and coolness in watching the expression, demeanour, and play of his opponent.

We will now suppose that we have taught him all we can, according to our lights, of the use of the foil; so we must advance a step further in the training which is to make him a "sabreur." We place in his hand the singlestick—this weapon represents the sword fairly in most points, excepting in weight and material. Its cuts, guards, points, and feints are precisely the same, and the stick, being a light weapon, is not likely to tire or disgust a beginner, and is from its lightness well adapted to the pupil who has but just passed through his course of fencing-drill. The soldier should undergo, after his fencing lessons are completed, a regular course of instruction in the stick practice; he should learn on foot in the fencing-school the cuts, points, guards, and the most effective feints, and should be thoroughly drilled in the practices: these latter we will presently discuss at length. When the instructor considers him sufficiently *au fait* of the various lessons, he should be made to perform independent practice, with a man whose fencing capabilities are just a very little better than his; or, which is much more beneficial to him, with a skilful, good-tempered, and judicious instructor. A lesson of independent practice from such a teacher is most advantageous, for he is able to detect and rectify many faults in the pupil's style, which would not be likely to occur in an ordinary class lesson, and it is the paramount duty of officers directing the school of arms to see that this is carried out.

When our pupil has received sufficient lessons and independent practice with the stick, we ought to arm him with the practice-sword; this weapon he should then be encouraged to use as much as possible; fortunately men who are really fond of the fencing-room require but little encouragement to keep to this weapon, for I have generally noticed, that after once or twice playing with it, they never seem to care for the singlestick again. As the stick, however, is the weapon with which the soldier must learn the rudiments of his play, I will endeavour to lay down, from past experience in some of the London fencing-schools, and taking as a basis the present Infantry Sword Exercise, a short and simple method by which he may easily acquire them.

The lessons are of two kinds—the single-rank lesson, consisting of simple and compound attacks and guards; and the double-rank lesson, consisting of the practices.

(21)

SINGLE-RANK LESSONS.

Fall in as usual.
Open distance from the right—march.
Eyes front.
Prepare for fencing lesson.
Draw swords.
Slope swords.

Engage . . . { Advance the right foot to the second position, keeping the chest well thrown forward, the shoulders back, and the head erect; the left hand resting on the hip with the fingers closed. Advance the right hand about six inches, lower the point of the stick obliquely across the body until it is about on a level with the left shoulder, and turn the back of the hand up, the part of the stick which represents the edge of the sword being directed outwards, the elbow to be covered by the guard of the stick.

SIMPLE ATTACKS. CUTS AND POINTS.

Care should be taken that all cuts are *completed* on the completion of the lunge.

Cut 1. . . . { Lunge to the third position, at the same time cut smartly out, diagonally downwards from right to left. This cut is intended for the left side of the opponent's head.

Engage . . .	Spring back to the second position, the body and stick to assume the above-described attitude.
Cut 2 . . .	Lunge, and cut diagonally downwards from left to right. This cut is intended for the right side of the head.
Engage . . .	As before.
Cut 3. . . .	Lunge, and cut diagonally upwards from right to left. This is intended for the inside of the opponent's leg.
Engage . . .	As before.
Cut 4. . . .	Lunge, and cut diagonally upwards from left to right. This is intended for the outside of the leg.
Engage . . .	As before.
Cut 5. . . .	Lunge, and cut horizontally from right to left. This is intended for the soft part of the left side.
Engage . . .	As before.
Cut 6. . . .	Lunge, and cut horizontally from left to right. This is intended for the right side.
Engage . . .	As before.
Cut 7. . . .	Lunge, and cut perpendicularly, for the centre of the head.
Engage . . .	As before.

(23)

Point in Quarte.	Turn the nails up, and, extending the arm, lunge out smartly. This point will be usually directed at the outside line.
Engage . . .	As before.
Point in Tierce.	Lunge out smartly, keeping the back of the hand up. This will usually be directed at the inside line.
Engage . . .	As before.
1*st position* .	With sloped sword.

Stand at ease.
Attention.

GUARDS.

All guards are to be made in the second position; the right foot must not be shifted back, for remember a mounted man cannot shift from a cut at pleasure. All cuts must be received on the forte of the sword.

Engage . . .	As before.
Guard 1 . .	Raise the hilt and bring it over to the left front, taking care not to draw the hand in towards the body; keep the point rather depressed, to receive cut 1, looking to the front over the right wrist.

Engage.

Guard 2 . . { Carry the hilt slightly to the right front, and elevate the point to receive cut 2.

Engage.

Guard 3 . . { Drop the point to the left front to receive cut 3.

Engage.

Guard 4 . . { Drop the point to the right front, carrying the hilt a little to the right to receive cut 4.

Engage.

Guard 5 . . { Raise the hilt to the left front about as high as the shoulder, and lower the point to receive cut 5.

Engage.

Guard 6 . . { Raise the hilt to the right front about as high as the shoulder, and lower the point to receive cut 6.

Engage.

Guard 7 . . { Raise the hilt to the front, the blade pointing across the body, and the point rather depressed, to receive cut 7.

Engage.

Against point the best guards are quarte, tierce, prime, and seconde.

COMPOUND ATTACKS OR FEINTS.

A feint is a false attack against any part of the opponent's body, intended to draw away his attention and guard, while the real attack is made at another part.

The feint is formed by showing the very slightest semblance of an attack—by a mere motion of the wrist towards a certain point *at the moment before the right foot rises from the second position*, while the cut or point is finished *at the moment the foot touches the ground in the third position or lunge*. In fact the opening must first be clearly made by the feint, and when so made must be pounced upon with precision and rapidity.

The swordsman, after selecting the best point to attack, should consider by what manœuvre he can put his opponent's blade into the most awkward position from which to recover to meet the real attack. The following are good cuts, and most likely to disable an adversary: 4 at leg (outside), 5 at left ribs, 3 at leg (inside), 6 at right ribs, 1 at neck, and 2 at neck.

The most effectual feints are, I think, as follow:—

Feint 1, at left neck	Cut 4, at leg.
„ 2, at right neck	„ 5, at left side.
„ 2, at right neck	„ 3, at leg (inside).
„ 4, at leg	„ 1, at left neck.
„ 5, at left side	„ 2, at right neck.
„ Point in quarte, at face	„ 6, at right side.

It is a good plan to make the pupil practise these

compound attacks at a dummy, say a sack filled with sawdust or sand, and placed upright; while the instructor must carefully observe that the above-mentioned fundamental rules are strictly carried out.

LESSON FOR THE RECEIPT OF A FEINT.

The feint being a movement intended to deceive the eye and shake the nerve of the opponent, it is necessary so to train the pupil that he may not be attracted by the false attack. To this end the instructor will place him at engaging distance, and explain that he is about to attack a named part of the body, using at the same time a feint in order to effect an opening; this will be repeated until the hand of the pupil ceases to be drawn towards the part menaced, and forms the guard against the real attack, when the instructor will name and work upon some other part in like manner. Subsequently, as a more advanced lesson, two different parts will be named, and the pupil directed to make a return hit after a successful guard, after the manner of the ensuing practices.

THE DOUBLE-RANK LESSONS.

These lessons are intended to be, as it were, a connecting link between the simple lessons of the cuts and guards, and the independent practice. They consist of four practices.

It should be observed that, as the point is the most effectual attack of the sword, and consequently one with which the soldier ought to become thoroughly acquainted, I introduce it as much as possible in the different practices.

These practices consist of a certain number of fixed cuts and guards; they must at first be performed by word of command, and when the men sufficiently understand the order in which the cuts, &c., come, they must work them, judging their own time. The benefit of these lessons is, that the men when performing them know what attacks and guards are to be made, and so gradually gain confidence in themselves, and at the same time learn how to make good return hits with speed and smartness.

The class will be formed as for the double-rank lessons with the foil, the men who are advanced and faced about representing the front rank.

1st Practice. Cuts and Guards.

Front rank will commence.
Engage.

Front Rank.	*Rear Rank.*
Cut 1 (at left neck).	Guard 1, cut 2.
Guard 2, cut 3.	Guard 3, cut 4.
Guard 4, cut 5.	Guard 5, cut 6.
Guard 6, cut 7.	Guard 7.

Engage.
Reverse the practice. Rear rank will commence.

(28)

2nd Practice.

Front rank will commence.
Engage.

Front Rank.	*Rear Rank.*
Cut 7 (head).	Guard 7, cut 3 (leg).
Guard 3, point tierce.	Guard prime (or 5th guard).

Engage.
Reverse the practice.   Rear rank will commence.

3rd Practice.

Engage.

Front Rank.	*Rear Rank.*
Cut 4 (leg).	Guard 4, cut 7 (head).
Guard 7, cut 1 (left neck).	Guard 1, point tierce.
Guard prime.	

Engage.
Reverse the practice.

4th Practice.

Engage.

Front Rank.	*Rear Rank.*
Disengage and tierce point.	Guard prime, cut 1 (left neck).
Guard 1, cut 4 (leg).	Guard 4, disengage and point tierce.
Guard prime.	

Observe that when the pupils perform these lessons judging their own time, the movements must be made as rapidly as possible.

When the men have thoroughly learned the above practices, they should be encouraged to play with each other independently with the singlestick, and on no occasion to be without masks; and as soon as they have by practice and experience become versed in the use of the stick, the steel practice-sword should be placed in their hands, and having arrived at this point, their loose play should be performed with no other or inferior weapon. This weapon has many advantages over the stick; its shape being that of the real sword, enables the soldier to gain the habit of cutting with the true edge. The weight too of the steel sword is nearer to that of the soldier's own weapon, and consequently, by its use, the muscles of his arm become strung up by constant practice to such a pitch as to enable him to handle his own heavy sabre with little or no fatigue, and this would not be the case were he to practise only with the light singlestick. Its hilt is roomy, and does not cramp or otherwise hurt the hand; the buffalo-hide stick-guards at present issued are so small as to impede the free play of the wrist, and even to cut the hand severely during loose play, and with such a weapon it is impossible to fence with either confidence or comfort. The stick is also a faulty weapon from the fact of its constantly twisting over the guard, and thereby causing a man to receive a sharp rap when he does not deserve it, than which nothing is so conducive to loss of temper. It is impossible for this to happen with the practice-sword.

RULES FOR INDEPENDENT PRACTICE WITH SABRE OR STICK.

1. No one to play, on any pretence whatever, without wearing a helmet.

2. Cuts and thrusts are not to be given too strongly; should men appear to be losing their temper, their play is to be stopped at once.

3. No two cuts or thrusts are to be made on the same lunge.

4. The opponents should not both strike at once; should this happen the cut or thrust given in the third position to be considered effective. But should both parties lunge, the hit to count to neither.

5. The act of crossing (and touching) the blades is a guarantee that both parties are ready. Any hit given before this is done, is not to be considered effective. The opponents should always engage out of distance.

6. A disarm to count as a hit to the party effecting it.

7. A hit is only considered effective when given with that part of the stick which represents the edge, or with the point.

8. In stick-play, no hit is to be made at the inside of the leg unless the players wear leg padding, a blow in that part being highly dangerous.

9. When playing with the practice-sword it is necessary to wear full padding, that is, helmet, double-jacket, gauntlet, body-pad, and leg-pad.

10. Players are strongly recommended to fence for a fixed number of hits, say 3, 5, or 7; this increases the interest in the play, and tends to make the men more careful in their fencing.

SWORD v. BAYONET.

To lay down precise rules for a combat between two weapons so thoroughly unequal as are these, is absolutely impossible; one can but offer suggestions.

The bayoneteer should keep his point rather low and to the left front, and always slightly in motion. He should be ready to pounce upon any opening shown, and should occasionally have recourse to feints in order to effect such an opening.

The swordsman should never attack direct, but should await and parry the thrust of the bayonet; the best guards being quarte, tierce, prime, and seconde.

He should always have his left hand ready to seize the musket after a successful parry, when his opponent would be practically disarmed.

www.ingramcontent.com/pod-product-compliance
Lightning Source LLC
Chambersburg PA
CBHW022345040426
42449CB00006B/729